WILD HEART
PEACEFUL SOUL

# Wild Heart, Peaceful Soul

*Poems and Inspiration to Live and Love Harmoniously*

J. Autherine

GIFT FOR:

_____

FROM:

_____

DATE:

_____

WILD HEART, PEACEFUL SOUL

©2018 by Autherine Publishing

Visit us on the Web at www.JanetAutherine.com

ISBN: 978-0-9912000-3-0

Library of Congress Control Number: 2018906779

*Autherine*
PUBLISHING

WILD HEART, PEACEFUL SOUL: POEMS & INSPIRATION TO LIVE AND LOVE HARMONIOUSLY - A PART OF THE GROWING INTO GREATNESS SERIES OF INSPIRATIONAL BOOKS.

# CONTENTS

# INTRODUCTION

*"I am made up of unexpressed emotions; they flow through my eyes, smile, touch, and most often, the pen."*

As a child in Jamaica, I spent a lot of time memorizing verses both in church and in school (songs, poems, written word). A child was considered very bright if she was able to memorize a long passage, and boldly walk on stage to recite it as friends and family cheered. As a rather shy introvert, I couldn't pull off recitation without feeling on the verge of a breakdown but I loved poetry and in my mind, I was on stage acting out every verse.

The first traditional poem that I remember memorizing was, "I Wonder Why the Grass is Green" by Jennie Kirby. After moving to the United States, I started reading everything that I could find by great authors, such as Dr. Maya Angelou. I Know Why the Caged Birds Sing touched me deeply and is still one of my favorite books. Her poems, "Phenomenal Woman" and "Still, I Rise" gave me the courage to walk confidently in the world. I believe that was when I started transitioning from writing about my day in my diary to writing free-form poetry. I started to understand the power of the written word, so every emotion that I couldn't verbally express, was expressed through my pen. I was most excited to write when a "heart" issue was involved - love, struggle, passion, heartache, unrequited love. I lead with my heart in almost every area of my life so the inspiration came often.

Books by Maya Angelou and Toni Morrison also sparked my love for issues that are close to the heart of women. As women, we spend our lives caring for others and putting the needs of others first. This often comes at a cost to our emotional and physical health and well-being. This is particularly true for women of color who are fighting to maintain a peaceful soul in the midst of political, racial and, societal dysfunction that breaks our heart on a daily basis. Many of the poems in the chapter, *Wild Heart*, deal with self-sacrificing behaviors - loving someone at the cost of our own emotional health, feeling unloved or unworthy of love, struggling with issues of abandonment and rejection, fighting losing battles with love, and drowning in despair. The chapter, *Peaceful Soul,* helps us find our way back to being the "Phenomenal Woman" that sister, Maya envisioned for all women.

Wild Heart, Peaceful Soul is dedicated to women everywhere who lead with their hearts. It is risky business for us because we feel deeply and love hard. It also means that we are prone to falling hard. Falling hard is easier when you have a peaceful place to land. Sometimes, we have to create that perfect landing place in our soul. Wild Heart, Peaceful Soul is the yin and yang of love. Let your wild heart run free, enjoying every mile of the journey, but also make sure that it knows how to find its way back home.

THE HEART'S JOURNEY

Years from now when I read my poetry,
I may not recognize myself,
but I will never be ashamed of my heart's journey;
of the loving,
of the giving,
of the kindness,
of the pain.

My heart fulfilled its purpose
to love
authentically
fiercely
passionately
and unconditionally.

Wherever you are in your journey, I hope that you have the freedom to let your heart run as wild as it can without sacrificing the peace that your soul needs. Never forget that self-love is the springboard for all the love that you give. When we love and care for ourselves, our vessel is full enough to pour into others. We have to commit to loving ourselves, fiercely, passionately and unconditionally.

# *I*

# WILD HEART

---

*"I am afraid that if I say that I am over you, the universe will call my bluff."*

## Quiet Storm

A quiet storm blew
through her life,
swept her off her feet
and then buried her
in an avalanche
of fallen leaves.

The ride was so thrilling
that she didn't realize how
hard she hit the ground
until her heart started to bleed;
he was already gone.

*"I always smile when I see your face. You are on my screensaver to remind me that happiness does exist."*

## The Weight of Your Presence

Joy is being in your space
but not speaking,
just feeling the weight of your presence,
occasional glances,
soul smiling,
feeling like all is right with the world,
even for a moment.

*"The mind is on a new journey;
the body had recovered; the
heart has healed but the
badass soul won't let go."*

## The Rebel Soul

I deleted all your photos,
removed them from my memory,
trained my heart not to love you,
my mind not to think of you… much

but

my soul still aches for you,
my soul wants to run to you,
my soul is waiting, quite impatiently,
to betray me.

*"I am an introvert but call
me anytime; that is how
much I love you."*

# I Don't Like People

When the dysfunction in the world
overwhelms my senses, I cling to you.

When I reject everything in my path,
I still choose you.

When my soul aches for solitude,
my heart wants to pull you closer.

When I crawl into my shell to hide,
you are the only comfort that I crave.

I choose you.

I don't like people, but I love you.

*"Love is an unbroken circle. Real love returns home, sometimes with familiar eyes, sometimes though a new soul."*

## Eternity Awaits

From the first time that I saw you,
it has always been you—
You can leave my life, physically
but you are always with me.
You have my DNA,
I have your DNA,
I carry it proudly.

Traveling mercies for your journey
but never forget the way home.
If we meet again,
it will be as if you never left.
If not in this lifetime,
eternity awaits.

*"She watched them stand at the edge of the pool. Hopeful. Arms outstretched. Smile. Wink. The water is warm. Waiting, waiting, waiting for one brave enough to dive in. Love doesn't have many heroes but love is worth the wait."*

## Hail Mary

"I love you" was a wish
A Hail Mary
An invitation to come in
Sit hard
Let your guard down
Show me the dark places
that only love can understand.

*"He kept lowering the bar but she was happy to dance under it. Although her compromising positions were breaking her body and spirit, she still cried when he dropped the bar and walked away."*

## Foolish Heart

You break my heart and mend it at the same time,
making me instantly forget any past hurt.
Blood rushes to the heart again,
washing away any caution.
Feeling alive again,
Ready to try again...
Unapologetically foolish.

*"They enjoyed a pitcher of beer. The relationship was over before they got to the bottom. She wasted six months trying to get a refill."*

## Ghosting

No goodbye
No clarity
Just the cold breeze of retreat
Familiarity becomes formal
Warmth disappears
Strangers again
Naked and alone
without even an emoji smile
to keep you warm.

*"I didn't realize that I was a sore loser until I lost you."*

## A Traitor

I begged, pleaded, even bribed my heart
to love someone else, but it would not move,
Its loyalty was damning to us.
I dragged it,
kicking and screaming away from you,
depriving it of the opportunity
to fall to pieces over you.
A traitor is what it called me.
It feared that my act of kindness would lead to its demise.
The heart can bounce back from brokenness,
but it cannot survive emptiness.

*"She wondered how much love she could give and receive before the inevitable rejection and heartbreak came."*

## Empty House

The are no photos of you because
you didn't want to be remembered,
but I miss you.
I miss everything about you.
You made no effort,
but just the unfiltered you was enough.
Just being in your presence was enough.
You were restless. I was home.
I miss home.

*"I wallowed in so much sorrow that my ancestors rose up to lift my head and straighten my shoulders; they raised me to be stronger."*

## An Empath's Sanity

They say that this little pill
is supposed to help me smell the roses.
It is supposed to help me enjoy the music of a waterfall,
roll on the ground with my dog
and smile back at children.
It is "normal" to dream of weddings and birthdays
and believe in happy endings.
The world is painted in white, pink and shades of gray,
but I only see the gray.

I am more clairvoyant than the rest of them...

There are people crying out in pain in my TV set,
and I am the only one who cares.
Laugh, cry but when the show is over,
leave your emotions on the couch—
Not me. I carry them with me.
The pain sticks to me like used chewing gum.
Can't change the channel because the voices
tell me that I am their only hope.

I pray for a world that has warm shades of brown, but the
tiny imperfections on the mirror block out any beauty.
Life doesn't feel like a gift that I can open.
My soul is trimmed and pruned like a suburban plant.
Find the strength to paint the madness white,
paste on a half-smile,
just enough to cover the sadness,
to deter the curious from questioning

my sanity.

*"I can find another love like you but
I can't find another friend like you."*

# Gone Too Soon

You were not cold,
although you pretended to be.
Your heart was warm, wild;
when you allowed yourself to feel, you felt deeply.

I understand because I am afraid of the cold,
afraid of rejection but was drawn to you.
No fear, just fascination... with every crooked line on your face,
the way your heart beat like it was afraid.
Your unfocused stare,
because when you made eye contact,
your heart revealed itself.
Your impulsive declarations of joy that gave me hope.

I felt called to protect everything in you.
There were so many layers of you to explore.
Gone too soon. I feel robbed.

*"She became accustomed to rejection so her anxiety started at hello."*

## I Love You. Goodbye

*Do you love me?*
I am afraid to answer that.
*Why?*

Your friendship is important to me;
I am afraid you will run.
*Our bond is unbreakable.*
Yes, I love you.
*Then, I must say goodbye. Love is freedom.*
Tears.

*"When you light a fire in someone's heart, don't walk away as it burns."*

## Lost Love

I am home...
Writing,
Crying,
Drinking,
Saying, damn you
to my heart for missing you so much.
Heartache,
Heartache,
Heartache...
When will this shit end?

*"She had to recover from living with someone who treated her like her very existence was reason to be angry."*

## Irretrievably Broken

Till death do us part shouldn't mean murder or suicide.
You were murdering me with your anger, lies, unkindness.
I was committing suicide by holding on to the sharp knife of your anger.
I was dripping in blood but the inner pain hurt more.
Heart shattered.
Mind filled with guilt, shame, confusion, and naive hope.
Soul echoing from emptiness.

The judge looked at my mangled hand and asked
"Are you sure this union is irretrievably broken?"
The God that lives in me, cognizant of its own mortality said "yes."

Till death do us part shouldn't mean murder or suicide.

*"Deep yearning isn't deep love; it is all the unmet expectations rising to the surface of your soul."*

# The Emotional Burn

That internal ache
that lights up the body
but clouds the mind.
You are within reach.
I could run to you… if you would let me
but instead, I burn
and wait
and burn
and wait
until you invite me in
to lock eyes
touch your lips with mine
feel the weight of your presence
die and be reborn in your arms
ride the emotional high
until the mind is clear, the soul is set free
with more time
to wait
and burn
and wait
and burn until
you invite me back in.

*"Is it weird that all I want from you is to know that you are alive? Knowing that you still exist in this world calms me."*

## Internal Wound

Anger is powerful.
It protects us from inflicting internal wounds.
Blame is assigned. Punishment is administered.
The heart, the mind, and the soul powerfully exhale,
free themselves from the negative energy
and prepare to live and love again.

It's been months since I exhaled.
I lost the power to feel anger towards you.
I only hurt inside.

*"I looked at you and only saw beautiful because legendary is the ability of a woman's mind to weave fields of roses from thorns."*

## Slayed

He doesn't love
He slays hearts
and places them on the shelf
with his other trophies
occasionally pausing to caress his prizes

His caress is so powerful
that the hearts stay,
eagerly awaiting the next touch and
taking bets on what condition the new
girl's heart will be in when it arrives.

*"It takes a deep and abiding love for yourself to have the patience to wait for the companion who is mentally healthy enough to see the beauty in your heart. No filters required."*

## Good Enough To Love

Fancy degrees
Skinny jeans
Summer body
Specks of food
Laughing at jokes
Hiding the intellect
Always kind, always loving, always giving
Compliment, compliment, compliment the ego

Still not good enough to be loved
by a heart that only sees its own shadows
and only dances to its own beat
Love yourself.

*"Just because 1 or 10 or 100 lovers do not love you, doesn't mean that you are unlovable. Your self esteem is not a prisoner to another's nefarious agenda. Learn the lesson, stand tall and move one step closer to the love that your heart desires."*

# The Con Artist

It was ordinary
Just another guy saying and doing the right things to get a girl
Getting the girl and then pulling away
Acting surprised that the girl fell for his two-step
The girl, not wanting to believe that she was conned,
continues to believe that what they had meant something

She tries to hold on to what they had before
He pulls further away
She downgrades to friends with benefits
Not her proudest moment

She tries to salvage just a friendship
Anything not to feel used and abandoned
Nothing
Silence
Blinders off
Reality sets in

She wasn't anything special
Extended self-flagellation
Senses regained
Self-esteem comes crawling back
She is indeed special, just not to him,
and that is okay. (Repeat.)

*"She calls but he doesn't pick up.
She texts but he doesn't respond.
She likes all his posts, loves all his
photos but he doesn't acknowledge
her existence. He doesn't care
that his face is on her screensaver
and etched in her heart."*

## Lost Friendship

I said that I wouldn't let you break my heart
but that was when my heart was above the clouds
when our wine glasses danced together
when your text was my constant companion
when you loved to cook for me and the sweet
taste of your sauce never left my lips
when I kissed you every time the elevator door closed

Losing your friendship broke my heart
My heart never intended to descend from the clouds.

*"Don't box the soul in; it
has many mates."*

## The Meetup

Dancing eyes
Fingers exploring her neck
Hand caressing her back
Her mind starts to race
drowning out the sound of the band
as it considers whether to reward bold moves
with a kiss or a rebuke.

Hell yea
Lean in
Touch his cheek
Meet his gaze
Drown out all the eyes at the bar
for a most exquisite kiss...
Chemistry.

*"We all hit rock bottom; sometimes, you bounce up fast, sometimes you crawl until you can straighten up and sometimes you have to lay there for a long time until you learn how to rise again."*

## Season of Her Discontent

She is no longer giving birth,
Her spirit is dying,
Unexplained tears.
Grieving and pain
have replaced nerves of steel.
It's the season of her discontent.

So many deaths: thyroid, uterus, hope.
Her heart is longing
and her soul is yearning
for things beyond their reach.
The mind is fighting
to keep the house of cards from collapsing.

It's the season of her discontent.
Gratitude no longer yields happiness,
She is no longer giving birth,
Her blessings are numbered,
so please appreciate the few cherry blossoms
that she has left to give. She clings to them, but for you,
she releases them with trembling hands.

Accept them with warmth, appreciation, kindness.
If you reject even one, you reject all that she is.
It is the season of her discontent
and she is not sure that her cherry blossoms
will bloom again in the spring.

*"Truth. You never completely heal from some heartbreaks. You are still worthy of giving and receiving love."*

## A Writer's True Love

When I think of you, I hurt
It is poetic, it is painful
I could forget and feel nothing
Turn the page and look at emptiness
Pain, sorrow, regret are fuel for my true love…
the pen

Without your pain, I don't write
I choose pain, I choose you.

*"Embrace the light, the
darkness, the peaceful spirit
and the madness."*

## Embrace All That You Are

I allow the pen to write freely but
don't always publish it's poison.
I allow the mind to travel to dark places
when I know my way home.
I am in control of my journey.
I own my darkness

*"Ready to feel again. Ready to trust again. Ready to love again. The heart gets knocked down but it does not stay down."*

## Time Heals

Your pain was special.
It imploded,
inhabited every pore,
made a woman lay on her back
and question her place in the world.

The pain is now gone.
I miss it.
I clung to it as long as I could,
reliving every prick of the pin,
but time healed me...
without my permission.

*"Her head was in the clouds
when she tripped over a stranger
and broke her heart."*

# Tough Love

You have lost Dick.
Move on.
That's what your subconscious
is telling you with dreams of infidelity
and hurt and pain
and anguish.

While you have been pining,
he has been traveling the world,
offering his prized possessions to someone else
and being joyfully claimed.

He was yours for a brief moment in time
No love was attached
You attached love to it because you are a lover.
You attached friendship, you clung,
you texted, you fantasized, you hoped.

You forced your mind to make connections
by obsessing over his photos, his slight words, his zero promises,
his fleeting touch, his deep but meaningless looks...

His story is not real.
He doesn't love and pretends not to feel.
Mourn the loss that you have created.
It wasn't authentic but it's still painful.
It still makes you cry in your dreams.

*"Let us never get so jaded by the complexities of life that we forget the sweetness, pureness, innocence of love at first bloom."*

## The Quiet Storm of Love

"Do you love me?" he quietly asks.
*"I love you*
*with every breath,*
*every heartbeat,*
*every shift of the wind.*
*You inspire every thought,*
*you occupy every dream.*
*Every time my soul awakes, it awakens for you..."*

"Yes," I quietly replied.

*"The pain broke through the skin, dismantled her pores, and ate away at everything that was once strong. She was laid bare with nothing to cling to."*

# Imperfect Vessels Need Love

Bitten by the sorrow of loneliness.
Feeling hopeless; hope has been
blocked by sadness,
blocked by fear,
blocked by tears.

They say
focus on friends,
focus on work,
focus on you,
your turn will come
when you are healed, a perfect vessel.

Don't tell me fables
in the midst of my anxiety,
in the midst of my pain,
in the midst of my sorrow.
Imperfect vessels need love the most.
Unloved is all that I feel.
It burns my soul.
I only have the strength to breathe.

*"I looked inside your heart and saw all scars. I wanted to heal them all but you had sharpened all the edges and I just walked away wounded."*

## Blind to Love

Wisdom failed me
I fell in love too quickly
Became fearful
The heart started pulling the strings
I couldn't get the blinders off to see all of you
To share all of me
Too busy trying not to lose you to be authentic
Two strangers in love
Hearts clinging but souls never connecting
Being in love is the enemy of love.

*"Your effect on me is mysterious. When I am mentally hiding under my desk, you appear on my screen, my heart breaks out in song, a smile travels to my ear and my dark clouds start to dance."*

## Smile In My Direction

You are beautiful.
Wide-rimmed glasses,
Sly smile, like to know a secret
that the world isn't smart enough to discover.
Your face comes alive with a boyish grin
when you tell a joke; your eyes sparkle.
Smile in my direction.

Below the perfectly pressed shirt and tie:
soft heart, soft skin. Vulnerability exposed with a touch.
When your hips swing, butterflies dance and petals are open.
Swing in my direction.

Kiss me again and again.
Surprising, endless kisses; deep, nuanced kisses.
Early morning kisses just as passionate as the night before.
Your lips weave a story that the heart never tires of hearing.
Weave it in my direction.

Daylight breaks, and a heart has been healed but duty calls.
Your expert hands are obligated to heal others.
Your smile, touch, kiss demand freedom.
When you walk to the door, turn around and
smile in my direction.

*"Be bold and very specific about your intentions. I requested a guy who is crazy about me but the universe just heard crazy."*

## Intentions

Not everyone who stumbles on our porch
comes for sweet tea.
The heart can't always discern the difference;
it just loves.
The mind has to be the leader.
It has to coax the heart into loving from afar,
setting boundaries that the heart cannot leap over.

*"Have the courage to speak your truth. Tears from uncertainty flow inward and pollute the body. Tears from lies burn longer, deeper, and shatter the self esteem. Tears from the truth create an explosion, then set you free."*

## Passing Time

He has my heart,
so that makes me a lousy date,
but his heart is unavailable so
I show up and smile and say all the right things,
but I'm just biding time until he texts again.

If you are lucky,
that may not be for a few weeks.
In the meantime, we can play house.
I can pretend that my heart isn't bleeding,
that I'm not thinking about his touch—

I'll understand if you leave.
I am sorry.
It's a bad bargain,
but I loved him first
and my heart won't forget.

*"Forgiveness, compassion and understanding are the deepest ways that you can touch and heal another human being.*

## Steel

Pain, tears before eyes of steel,
Sweet revenge for deeds unknown,
A hardened heart.
Wished I understood why there was no immunity
from the deep freeze in your soul.

In days gone by, there were glimpses of summer.
Pain, fear has erased all but the bitter.
A glimmer of hope but the aftertaste lingers.
A severe reaction to perceived danger.

Fight or flight? Why not both?
Fight with the pen throwing daggers from afar.
Precision comes with practice.
Vengeance is mine but remind me why.

The body and mind self-corrects if allowed.
The danger has passed.
Let go of the poisoned pen
Free yourself. Free me
from the cold steel that pierces us both.

*"When you understand your inner self — your passions, motivations, moral code and vulnerabilities, you don't have to blow in the wind of someone else's expectations; you can stand firm in your own truth."*

# *Misunderstood*

I am so misunderstood.
Nothing I do is considered good.
Right is wrong and wrong is right.
Doesn't anyone understand my plight?

I lie in bed and think of you
and all the things that you want me to do.
A million thoughts swirl in my head.
I am sick of tossing and turning in this bed.

How good it would feel to yell and scream,
but these bold emotions happen only in my dream.
So I close my eyes and pray for sleep to come,
but who am I really running from?

Will tomorrow bring self-reflection?
Can I really find peace while looking in your direction?
A wise woman understands that her butterfly and caterpillar are one.
Not looking outside for validation when there is internal work to be done.

*"Failure is not trying, not giving, not loving. Your connection didn't last long but it wasn't failure. Sometimes, two ships pass in the night, briefly collide and keep sailing towards their destination; your collision just moved you closer to your purpose."*

## The Heart Surrenders

My soul made a connection
and desperately reached for your heart.
The heart was hot, then lukewarm, then cold.
The connection was thrilling.
The ache of separation was unbearable.

Walls,
no-access signs, and
silence are the most effective forms of rejection.
Heart ached, tears flowed.
Walls caved in.
Worth questioned.

Forcing a moment of reckoning,
Fight for love alone or
flight for the heart to survive.
Chase halted.
Passion ended.
Defeat reluctantly accepted.
Sadness sets in.

There were no breakthroughs.
Your story,
still a mystery.
Not wise enough to read the tea leaves
in order to understand what you needed,
so I just tried to give you the best of me.

But it wasn't enough.
Your soul found its joy outside of me.
I'm so sorry that I failed
when failure wasn't an option.
I really tried to be the light
that warmed your heart.

*"Love is not blind but if the heart has to choose between pain and loneliness, it will choose pain every time."*

## Vulnerable Heart

You were not right for me,
I was not right for you.
I was willing you settle,
you were not.
Your heart has never been broken,
my heart has been shattered,
delicately mended
still vulnerable —
You saved me from myself.

*"Infatuation goes dormant in times of a storm. Lust withers. Broken hearts and broken souls are created by the inability to wait for true love."*

## Love Game

Where can I go to buy a little love?
To have someone smile at me with his eyes,
touch my face, softly,
caress my cheeks,
hold me in a warm embrace.
See me, not see through me.
Tell me that he loves me
and pretend to mean it...

*"Inhale. Exhale. Meditate.
Center the emotions. Maintain
the delicate balance between
loving him and loving yourself."*

## The Mirror of Love

He loves her only because she loves him
so
she has to love him deeply,
passionately,
with great care,
so that the wind is always blowing on their backs
and no storm clouds arise,
because
*his* love is only a reflection of her own love for him,
and his love gives her a reason to breathe.

*"The love that you give always comes back to you but not always from the person that you expect. Keep loving."*

# Reclaiming My Heart, Again

I can't love again,
my heart is too vulnerable,
but loving was my favorite thing to do—
it was meant for me,
it was my gift;
the one thing that I knew that I could do well.
There were no insecurities.

But there was a shift in the heart
Pain no longer just passed through,
it lingered and left footprints.
It's hard to tell when the change happened...
Was it a single blow
or a thousand pin pricks?

The heart became fearful,
shivering,
tiptoeing around love,
then clinging,
going behind my back
and loving indiscriminately.

Searching for security,
believing attraction was intention,
breaking at will.
Too many failed attempts,
too many rejections
to be fixed.

I can't love again.
Too many battles lost,
the scar tissue is too extensive,
the heart is too damaged to heal,
but the mind is powerful;
it can reclaim my heart.
I can find my own security.

# II

# PEACEFUL SOUL

*"Your greatest weapon is the pen.*
*Write your own happy ending."*

# The Princess Takes the High Road

Believing all the fairytales, she waited patiently for her prince to return.
She continued on the low road for as long as she could
before realizing that the high road was the only way to rise;
the only path to the castle.
She sharpened her weapons,
slayed through the self-doubt,
cut the fear from her heart, and
trimmed all the edges that were blocking her vision.

With a clear vision, she wrote her own ending. *"The princess bravely scaled the walls of the castle. As she rose to the top, she created a path for the other young ladies who would follow and placed a beacon on the top of the castle to light their path. The End."*

*"Sisters, let us embrace our femininity, our vulnerability, our humanity. We are sometimes strong, sometimes fragile, but always perfectly made."*

## Her King

She is not passive but she is peaceful.
She is strong but she has vulnerabilities.
She wants to be the boss at the office
but not the boss of you.

Bring her your strength.
Empower her.
She wants to feel your masculinity.
Grow taller around her.

Inhabit the earth, reach for the sky.
Show her your power.
Spread your feathers like the male bird.
Make your inner beauty shine for her.

Her shoulders are already heavy,
so just for tonight,
leave your insecurities at the door.
Don't shed empty tears around her,
unless you plan to catch them
and use them to water her spirit,
her dreams, your love for her,
your passion for only her.

Allow her to exhale in your presence.

*"She writes the words that she longs to hear and carves them in her memory so that they automatically replay when she needs to love and care for herself just a bit more."*

## Strong Sisters Unite

My sisters, we are standing in the quicksand of
political, racial, relationship and other societal dysfunctions
Bravely declaring our strength and struggling to
hold it together but at what cost
We have nothing to prove; let us protect our minds & bodies

Our strength is being used against us
Our ability to be the fixer in every situation masks
our humanity, our femininity, our vulnerability
Let's not wait until we can't breathe to try to escape;
if we delay the healing, our scars will be permanent

The world knows that we are strong because
our strength is legendary
We are Harriet Tubman, Michelle Obama, and Rosa Parks.
We are Oprah Winfrey, Nanny, and Mae Jameson
We are Shirley Chisholm, Portia Simpson and Maya Angelou
We have birthed a nation, rescued slaves, built empires,
traveled to space and written our place in history

Survival is not enough; we were built to rise
Let us take each other's hand in love and support
Embrace our vulnerabilities
Embrace our humanity
Heal our hearts and minds
Escape from negativity is not failure
Self-preservation is not weakness
Strong Sisters, together we are stronger; together we rise.

*"Peace is love in its most
graceful state."*

## While We Wait

While we wait for our calling, our job is to be useful.
Let us build a mansion with pearly gates
and streets paved with gold in the depths of our hearts
Let us welcome in saints and sinners,
the beaten and the downtrodden,
the lost and the broken.
We are all human beings,
taking our own path to the same destination.

We will pool our tears and conspire to live life on earth
boldly, freely, joyfully, lovingly, peacefully—
Alone, each teardrop falls painfully to the ground.
Together, we have the resilience of the ocean.

*"Focus on the powerful footprints
that you are leaving in the sand."*

## Your Heart Belongs to the Mission

You are searching for love but it's not your turn—
It's another woman's turn to be starry-eyed,
heart aglow,
soul on fire,
pouring everything into another.

You have a purpose to fulfill;
It can't be done with stars in your eyes.
It can't be done with a distracted mind.
It can't be done with a divided heart.
In this moment, your heart belongs to the mission.

*"She felt the love in her bones
long before it reached her heart."*

## Your Heart is Protected

There is no ring on your finger,
but I have placed a ring around your heart.
You are always loved,
You are always protected.

The ring on your finger may never come.
Stop looking for it to validate the perfection that I have made.
You have already been stamped: God's property.
Stop whining. Fix your crown and go rule.

*"I fully embrace you. My life is better with you in it. I welcome you into my life with open arms."*

## Borrowed Time

I don't want to leave my hat on,
I want to take it off,
and get comfortable.
Put my feet on the center table,
leave my wine glass in the sink…
I want to feel at home.

No anxiety about leaving,
no side glance for clues
about when my time is up.
No worn out welcomes,
no uncomfortable goodbyes,
no relief that I am going home.

Have you forgotten anything?
Have you left any clues?
Pick up your heart,
I will pick up your bags.
Be sure to call me when you get home.

Can I walk you to your car?
No, I know the way.
This road is well-traveled
but my feet are tired of walking the same plank.

*"She leaves relationships
only when the hurt starts to
penetrate her bones."*

## Shared Space

Snakes, iguanas, alligators
all inspire fear for just being
beautiful, carefree, alive.
Surviving, thriving in shared space.
Feared, fearing in shared space.
Your freedom, my freedom intertwined.
Both looking to be free,
To peacefully share this land of liberty.

*"Love takes great pride in
rising to the challenge of loving
you in the most vulnerable
places of your heart."*

# The Male Bird

My gift to you is freedom
from the anxiety that comes from seeing me,
from the silent echoes of responsibility.
My vulnerability is best left for days
gone by when women and children first
was a sign of strength.

Close your eyes and sail to a place
where silence is still golden,
where your brilliance is unquestioned,
where talk of art and music is for the genius of the world,
where the male bird's role is to be pretty.

*"Love says, I have her in the palm of my hands and I will massage away any doubts and any fears until she stands confidently, and securely in my love for her. Ego says, "I have her in the palm of my hands and I will manipulate her until she is weak, fearful and totally dependent on me; only then can I be certain of her love for me. Choose love."*

## *Follow the Love*

Follow the love.
It is a peaceful path.
There is no climbing up dangerous terrain,
battling dragons and demons along the way,
carefully tiptoeing over hidden landmines.

Follow the love.
It doesn't hurt.
You don't have to change yourself to receive it.
It accepts that you are perfectly made.
No permission is needed to travel confidently in its world.

Follow the love.
You will recognize it by its non-resistance,
its warm embrace,
its offer for you to abide in its presence,
its sheer joy in being found.

*"The answer to why I love you is...just because you exist. It is not complicated but it is the best kind of love."*

## Wakanda Love

I want to
rise every morning with my heart
beating next to yours,
wipe any doubt or fear from your eyes,
infuse your spirit with love and awaken
the Black Panther in you.

I want to
anoint you with oil, stimulate your senses,
remind you of your strength, agility, stamina, genius,
make you feel your super human powers.

I want to
nourish you with the potions of our ancestors,
fill your veins with euphoria,
watch the God in you rise up.

I want to
be caught up in your rapture,
always by your side with my spear in hand,
ready to protect your heart and your throne,

fiercely serving you in our Wakanda.

*"There are two sides to every love story and every action or inaction causes the universe to slightly shift. Our hearts are fragile; love kindly and unselfishly."*

# The Love Life of A Book

I. *The Avid Reader*: She was a book lover's dream
and there was nothing that he loved more than books
This is the one that would add meaning to his life
He took her to the cafe and read her while enjoying
his favorite glass of red wine,
but he wasn't ready to purchase her
She was special but he was afraid
There were so many free books available online;
maybe he could swipe through their pages a few more times
before committing to a purchase that would change his way of life
Her words leaped off the pages with excitement when he touched her,
reassuring him that he had time to browse and return for her
So he placed her high on the shelf
where no other reader would find her,
and no other hands would touch her
Reluctantly, he walked away.


II. *The Good Book*: My pages are filled with fairytales
but I have never lived them
When he touched my pages, all the words
between my hard exterior came to life
He took me to the cafe and devoured my stories
while enjoying his red wine; he said it was the perfect evening
but surprisingly, he returned me to the shelf,
placed me higher so that
I could see him reading other books
but was powerless to intercede
My pages turned yellow from jealousy and began
to fall apart until the reader with the wide rimmed glasses walked in
He said that he was a birdwatcher
and could spot beauty from afar
He couldn't leave without such an exquisite find
I now rest comfortably by his bedside.
He reads a few pages every morning
and handles me with great care
Appreciated, treasured, loved
but the Avid Reader's wine glass left a stain inside of me
and I am never able to completely forget his touch.

*"If peace flows like a river, may it flow into the ocean of our souls."*

## Solitude

An hour alone is all I need.
Don't make me feel like this is greed.
I have reached into my mind, body and soul
and poured out every piece of me; now I am cold.

Hey there girl, isn't there more you can give?
Yes, but let me take a few extended breaths so that I can live.
This kind of love is a consuming fire.
I can't always keep up as you take me higher

I would like to wrap my arms around myself
and find that inner peace that only comes from first loving oneself.
This craving comes from deep within my soul.
There is no escaping it,
I can only smile as it unfolds.

*"At our core, we all want to be
needed and we all want to be
given the gift of trust. Statements
such as, I love you but I don't
trust you and I want you but I
don't need you are tiny roadblocks
to unconditional love."*

## Appreciation from the Universe

She will walk into welcoming arms or be content to sit in solitude.
Her hands are weathered from a lifetime of service.
Always extended to hug, care for, toil, fix every broken spirit.
For now, they will rest by her side
sometimes hanging freely,
sometimes fist clenched,
sometimes resting protectively on her heart,
sometimes joined together in prayer.
Always ready to rise again for the warm embrace of love.

When the stars need to be aligned
and the sun needs to shine brighter,
the universe will gently reach for her hands,
and hold her in a loving embrace
It understands her need to be appreciated for lighting
up the world with her touch.

*"The anger that is directed at you is not about you; what you are experiencing is the outpouring and overflowing of someone else's pain. Engage only after you have clothed your mind, body and soul in protective garment."*

# The Gift of Trust

I can't compete with the voices in your head
that tell you that everything is dread.

Freedom's light grows dim.
Why is it so hard to find peace within?
My own light is blowing in the wind,
trying hard to cling to its torch.

Can a tree thrive without its roots,
unassisted by sunshine?
A tree needs sunshine and rain.
What if only the rain came
and saturated the tree to its core?

There are no winners in imaginary battles.
Heart, mind, soul are all fighting.
Nine rounds of purgatory,
and the inner conflict devours its fighter.

Just once, allow me to love you unconditionally.
No questions, no doubts, no fear of rejection.
Accept a genuine smile without suspicion,
and a warm hug with no reservations.

Give me and yourself the gift of trust.

*"Being in love is the enemy of authentic love. It is a drug that makes your knees weak, your words accommodating and your body conforming to his will. Your true self is buried under the fear of losing the high."*

## Mature Love

My friend, can I share my love with you?
Can I hold both your hand of friendship and your heart?
Calm breezes blow and peaceful waters flow when I am with you.
My heart beats to a sweet, steady rhythm;
it doesn't race like that of a teenage love.

I pray that peace is enough for you
because there is comfort in the strength of your hands
and the certainty in your touch.
You are a creature of habit and your gaze never leaves me.
In our season, predictability is as meaningful as passion.

All my shooting stars collided leaving deep wounds,
but my wounds don't scare you
because your heart has been
both a wounded warrior and a medic.
As I sit in my low place and tell battle stories,
you place a crown of understanding
on my head because your believe that scars are to be honored.

If we are brave enough to be both friends and lovers,
I offer peace, understanding, and the freedom
to be a house sparrow or a soaring eagle.
Our forever is predictable only in its unpredictability.
Friendship guides our steps;
love will sprinkle stardust in our path.
I will always journey with you,
as your friend and with your permission,
your lover.

*"Love wins every, single, time
when we join hands and fight
for it just like it fights for us.
Even islands are connected by
water. Nature knows that without
connection, there is no survival."*

# The Art of Loving a Broken Vessel

A broken vessel needs love the most
Repair it with gentle hands and a kind heart
Apply patience to the bumps and rough edges
Fill the vulnerable places with love
Turn its broken pieces into perfectly imperfect art
Treasure the masterpiece that you have restored.

*"Love has the soul of a super hero; sometimes, it enjoys appearing right before all hope is lost in order to remind humanity of its power."*

## Love and Politics

I couldn't breathe.
My heart was on the verge of breaking,
Despair began to take hold.
The light of love was a fading shadow.

Then,
out of many one people, love appeared.
Through acts of kindness, love appeared.
Through hands joined tightly, love appeared,

reminding us that in the midst of anxiety,
in the midst of pain,
look beyond the sadness,
rise above the fear.

Through open hearts, love will appear.
Through understanding, love will appear.
Fight if you must, but don't despair.
Join hearts together and love will always appear.

*"The universe is fighting over my heart; today, the devil is dancing in the winner's circle."*

## Above It All

Today, I forgot to breathe.
The air was suspended between my throat and nose.
Frozen in anticipation of…
War and death,
famine and starvation,
rape and murder,
pride and pain,
fear and gridlock,
spam and debt,
depression and loneliness,
sadness and tears.

Tomorrow, I will turn off
the radio,
the television,
the internet,
negative people

Instead, I will take flight
above the clouds
where the air is thin
and I don't have to remind myself to breathe.
I will just look out the window of life as it crashes by,
descending only when I am in control
of each breath, each heartbeat, each emotion—
Everything that has meaning.

*"I am afraid that I am happier alone. Love me without expectations and I will love you without promises."*

## Free to Love

Let us love side by side.
No eye contact,
no deep, penetrating glances.
Hearts chatting without the need to shout,
Occasionally touching shoulders,
interlocking fingers, rubbing cheeks,
but no poetry,
no promises.

The heart isn't held hostage,
forced to beat faster than its capacity,
forced to prove itself daily.

*"Keep the love and give me peace.*
*I have no use for deceitful eyes*
*and a heart that betrays."*

## The Yellow Rose

Not every day is Valentine's Day.
Some days are for quiet reflection
on how your heart is not leaping but also not breaking,
on how much peace is in your world since she came along,
reflecting on the empty spaces that have been filled.
Wondering how and when you became so happy without drama.

If your scars were hidden, this would be a day for flowers,
Shakespearian words, fireworks…
but your heart has been broken, mended,
broken again, patched,
always vulnerable, always worn on the outside—
never healed… until now.

Today is a day for deep gratitude,
quiet tears and maybe a single yellow rose.

*"She came for love; she stayed for friendship. She lost both love and friendship."*

## Restless Souls Fly Away

Take what you can from a brief connection.
Don't make him your everything.
You may be his nothing
but that's not a reason to grieve,
because the connections
that illuminate the soul the most are brief
and the impact itself can't be erased.
The wind blew two restless souls together,
and only one held on tightly,
so you were blown apart—
Free to blow in the wind again,
To find a connection that clings,
One that can persuade your restless soul
to enjoy being on the ground again.

*"The voice in her head said:
Imperfect, unlovable, victim,
defeated, hide. The voice in her
heart said: Kind, peaceful, gentle
soul, easy to love, winner. Release
the insecurities and reclaim your
heart, your purpose, your peace."*

## Reclaim Your Heart

I was in the valley of despair,
waiting,
hoping,
praying
that you would see my worth,
that this would be the day
that you would acknowledge that I am your light.

I was not alone in the valley.
I found sisters with
dashed hopes,
deferred dreams,
fallen crowns,
self-inflicted wounds
existing in a broken place—
alive but not living.

Sisters,
look up, reach up!
Your crowns are damaged but not broken.
Shake off the self-hate.
Grab hold of self-worth
and walk out of the valley of despair.

Your walk may be unsteady but you won't fall.
Robe your self-esteem in royal garments.
Fiercely guard it from the enemy of loneliness, self-doubt.
Don't look for permission or validation to shine.
Bow to the reflection in your own mirror.
Reclaim your heart.

*"The heart just wants to love. Set it free. It knows that love is freedom, and freedom is peace."*

# God's Work is Done

I release you
in the mighty name of Jesus,
so that my heart and soul can stop
arguing over whether it was right to love you
and live in unity again.
Thank you for your light,
Thank you for your darkness,
Thank you for relighting the fire
in me that was on the verge of extinction.
My heart has purpose again,
my soul has peace again.
God's work has been done.

*"I wanted to love you in strength
but you touched my heart and all
my insecurities and vulnerabilities
came rushing out. Vulnerable to
the bone, I was too weak to have
a fighting chance with you."*

## You Were My Reflection

You were my mirror.
I looked past my own reflection
and I only saw you.
The perfect version of me
was the one that made you happy.

I am no victim.
I wanted to live in your shadow.
Your strength inspired me.
Your approval validated me.
It pushed me to achieve,
Disapproval, real or perceived
left me wondering how to be a better version of me

Fierce. Badass. That's what they call me.
Strong on the outside
and vulnerable on the inside but pushing through,
looking beyond the mirrors that are everywhere
to finally see me—
But even now,
I secretly hope
and pray that I didn't fail you.

*"She is a beautiful, powerful badass who sometimes falls apart inside after she drops her bags by the door and tosses her stilettos. Her vulnerability at night helps her to rise stronger in the morning."*

## Strong. Black. Woman

Hold on to a shred of dignity.
Scream inside.
Let the tears fall behind closed doors.
You are your mama's child
and she is a proud black woman.

She would be disappointed
if she knew that your heart breaks so easily.
That you blow in the wind
when she raised you to be strong.

Strong. Black. Woman.
Each word is non-negotiable,
so swallow hard,
steady yourself,
and carry on.

*"Stop saying that it takes a village and be the village."*

# The Strength of a Single Mother

Your shoulders are heavy,
but you stand tall and raise your head high,
knowing that you are raising kings and queens,
future leaders of the world.

You are pounding the pavement,
kicking butt, making it look easy
but we know better;
we know the struggle,
we understand the pain.

You are sometimes joyful.
sometimes fearful,
saying quiet prayers,
crying silent tears,
working miracles with limited resources.

We see you,
We respect you.
We are proud of you,
We have your back.
The road feels lonely
but you are not alone.

*"She pulled herself up from the rubbles and turned her pain into beautiful poetry. Each of her scars tell her story. She will not hide them to please anyone. Love all of her or leave her."*

## The Poet

I am not that strong
but my words are more powerful than I am.
My soul is drowning under the weight of my own insecurities,
my heart is often broken and my mind desperately
struggles for the right words, often failing,
but I hope that the words that I write
with a vulnerable heart
are strong enough to lift your spirit,
awaken your consciousness
and push you to the edge of your greatness.

*"The day that she declared, 'I will love my own darn self!' and walked away from it all."*

## Clothed in Love

I sew a garment with love
It keeps me warm
It reminds me that I matter
It reminds me of my best day
It fits me regardless of my size
It can cover me from head to toe with peace

The hood goes up to drown out negativity,
hide from a bad hair day,
find peace when the mind is overwhelmed,
and to bask in the feel and sound of silence

It is stitched with threads of hope
It covers a broken heart, abuse, disappointments
It provides comfort when I am feeling "less than"
It keeps me warm when the world gets cold

The garment of love knows what my heart needs
It is stitched with the fabric of my life
and it makes me feel as whole as the day before I was born —
the day before I faced the world and first cried out in pain.

*"He said, 'Break my heart one last time.' She refused. That was the heartbreak."*

## Waiting for Spring

The flowers in her garden faded under your care
Whenever they were on the verge of dying, you poured a bit of water
Just enough to raise her petals
Just enough to revive hope of blossoms in the Spring
Her flowers were never in full bloom but like a perennial,
she always waited patiently for an opportunity to try again.

*"A key is a symbol of openness; it gives the ones that we love access to our hearts, lives and homes. We can be open to walking a few miles with the ones that we love even if we don't understand every step of their journey."*

# Keys to Love, Peace & Understanding

I. Key to Love

The night that we met, he gave me the key to his heart
They felt heavy but I understood rejection, so I didn't say no
It was only the beginning of the heart's journey
but the key welcomed me
on board and assured
me that love would be traveling with us.


II: Key to Peace

Welcome to my home; love lives here
It is my safe space
I may not be able to face the world with you
but please take this key
and visit often.


III: Key to Understanding

She was on a journey that he didn't understand
Blowing in yesterday's wind
Her eyes told him that her heart wouldn't stay
and that her feet had never felt solid ground
But her soul called out to him
so he gave her the key to his heart and home
so that while her heart traveled,
her soul was always anchored in his love.

*"Our souls connected and
are having a love affair that
neither of us approve of."*

# Riding High

Riding on your high horse above the drama,
looking at all the little people living and loving recklessly,
wondering how they lost their self-esteem and moral high ground.

Distracted by self-righteousness,
you lose control of the reins
The horse takes off down a dimly lit path,
where there are complexities and grey areas and seductions.
You fall but surprisingly don't feel the pain so you linger,
enjoying the view from below,
tasting the depravity,
finally meeting the devil inside.

Shaken. Scared. Ego subdued.
You claw your way back up,
shaking off the dust, absorbing the shame,
fully aware of your humanity.
The horse is the same
but it doesn't recognize its rider.

*"The Wild Heart wants promises of forever. The Peaceful Soul just wants harmony in the present."*

## Forever is Fast Approaching

We are on the shorter end of forever.
Old enough to have loved foolishly, recklessly, fearfully
and shed a few tears, broken a few hearts.
Not too old to love passionately,
Too old for anything south of amazing.
We have earned the right
to proudly wave the single forever flag,
in peace, happiness, contentment.

But forever is fast approaching.
Consider giving love one more try.
It is not too late to dive into love.
This time, no loving on the surface.
No more fear, no puzzles to solve.
All our cards are face up on the table.

Grab what life and love has left
and love hard.
One more time.

*"One the verge of finding love, fear arrived to remind her that at her age, broken hearts don't easily mend."*

## Put on the Armor of Peace

45 is the age that I decided that peace
was my most treasured gift.
I dropped my weapon,
practiced passive resistance,
and put on the armor of self-love and self-protection.

Peace starts from inside
but only if you shield yourself from
negative news,
negative people,
hurt people who hurt people,
emergencies that are not of your own making.

Don't hide from the world
but don't absorb its negative energy.
Practice mindfulness.
Spread love and kindness when safety can be preserved.
Don't ever hesitate to guard your peaceful soul.

*"Next time I cry, it won't
be because I have fallen in
love and can't get up."*

# Baggage

We met online, the air was light; the conversation lighter
He couldn't see the bags that almost buried me
Too anxious to meet, we texted for months
Told him that something was weighing me down;
it was restricting my path to him.

Occasionally, I would look at the bags wondering if
I had the courage to leave them but my mind resisted;
it didn't want to be free.

These bags have been packed and unpacked
Every garment inside has been worn and re-worn
Sorted again to see if the load could be lightened
Still, they weighed heavily on my shoulders

Nothing inside fit but I still remember when they did…perfectly
The stories played again and again in my head, with added drama;
the good times were great and the sad times were heartbreaking.

The day that he knocked on the door, I was trying on the dress that
I wore the last time that I loved myself
In the midst of anxiety, fear, and despair, I threw all my bags at his feet.
They were so heavy that he couldn't walk away
"I'm going to help you with these," he said.

He dumped them all in the trash as I sat and cried
The pain that kept me warm was gone
As he took the final bag to the trash,
I opened the blinds and a glimmer of hope set in.

*"In the eyes of God, you are light and easy to carry. I pray that your journey will always be easy and those that are placed in your path will embrace you with arms extended, wanting to give so much more than they will receive."*

# The Heart and Soul of Africa

My heart belongs to Africa
Her essence brought my soul back to the motherland
I walked on earth that already recognized my footprints,
planted seeds in fertile soil and heard the music of
my ancestors in her voice

She wore the confidence of every woman that raised me
I took her hand and carried her through fire
as repentance for all the sisters and brothers that I couldn't
love while I was waiting for her

She spoke in tongues that made me feel invincible
Made me want to protect her and her entire village
Rule like the kings and queens that were my ancestors
before colonialism tried to hunch their backs
and break their spirits

Africa reclaimed my heart
Beckoned me to return to my roots
Asked for my forgiveness
Forgave all my past transgressions
and gave me back my crown.

*"Our roots are the invisible hands that shape how we live, love and how confidently we walk in the world. Our roots are not always visible so we have to dig deep into our souls to discover them, understand how they have been planted, nurture them and learn to love every branch."*

## You Are Worthy

My sisters, speak your truth
Embrace and love your whole being
Fiercely guard your heart
Be weary of anyone controlling your life in the name
of God, the devil and everything in between.

Clothe yourself in optimism
Banish all forms of negative energy
Take time for mental and physical healthcare
Self-care is Life-care
Proudly recognize that you are the President,
CEO and Keynote Speaker of your life
Nothing important to you works without a healthy you
You are worthy of love, worthy of abundance and
worthy of a healthy life. Always.

# ABOUT THE AUTHOR

J. Autherine is a poet, author and proud introvert. Her writing speaks to the heart of women globally. She was born in Jamaica and currently resides in Florida.

Her poem, The Poet, perfectly captures the vulnerability of her soul and her poetry.

## *The Poet*

I am not that strong
but my words are more powerful than I am.
My soul is drowning under the weight of my own insecurities,
my heart is often broken and my mind
desperately struggles for the right words, often failing,
but I hope that the words that I write with a vulnerable heart
are strong enough to lift your spirit, awaken your consciousness
and push you to the edge of your greatness.

Follow her for daily poems and inspiration.
IG: https://www.instagram.com/j.autherine/

www.ingramcontent.com/pod-product-compliance
Lightning Source LLC
Chambersburg PA
CBHW071459070426
42452CB00041B/1929